UTAH

Moments in Time

BY MICHAEL WICKES

Produced by:

MICHAEL WICKES PHOTOGRAPHY
PO Box 3313
Hailey, ID 83333
www.wickesphoto.com
(208) 788-4888

Edited by Colleen Daly.
Designed by Emilia Burchiellaro.
Map illustration by Blake Thornton.

Permission acknowledgments:

Page 37: Reprinted with permission
of Don Congdon Associates, Inc.
© 1968 by Edward Abbey, renewed 1996
by Charlie Abbey.

Page 63: Reprinted with permission, from
the book EVERETT RUESS: A VAGABOND FOR
BEAUTY, ed. W. L. Rusho. Salt Lake City:
Gibbs Smith, Publisher [Peregrine Smith
Books] 1983.

Printed by Tehabi Books.

First Edition
ISBN 1-931688-22-2

To order a copy of this book:
www.wickesphoto.com
(208) 788-4888

ACKNOWLEDGEMENTS

Among the many businesses and people who have helped me

during the production of this book, I am particularly indebted

to the following: Black Diamond, John Botkin (Photocraft),

Emilia Burchiellaro, Colleen Daly, Wayne Eastep, Brian Formusa,

Mark Kashino, Ray Lusty, Pawan Mehra, Jo Murray, Gerry

O'Toole, Patagonia, Bill Smith, Wolf Skis, Barbara Wilson,

Andy Wolcott, my family and, most of all, Kirsten Dougherty.

CONTENTS

Moments in Time

It is so hot. Even the Anasazi petroglyphs I photographed earlier seemed tired of the solar attack. A timid breeze has failed to displace the smothering heat, so I suggest to the sun that it take the rest of the day off. The request is denied.

Seeking relief under a little juniper, I put dinner on the stove as a storm moves across Monument Valley towards my camp below Cedar Mesa. Keeping an eye on the psychotic lightning that's snapping down closer and closer, I anxiously brush a patina of red dust off one of my battered Leicas. Dusk's stillness is worried by a moaning breeze, which suddenly detonates into a dervish of wind and sand. Away flies dinner.

As thunder groans, a biblical shaft of sun reaches from under the clouds and, for less then a minute, the mesa walls radiate a molten glow. I lock this magnificent scene on film.

It was in this setting that I began the photographs for *Moments In Time*. During the next six seasons I found myself following a loosely-aimed trajectory across Utah, with luck and serendipity as my guides. Along the way I was regularly ambushed by those quiet places and ordinary people that are the essence of Utah. Often just a fragment of a scene caught my eye. "Stop," someone or some place would say without speaking, "take another look." And so I would stop. And look again. And shoot.

GETTING HERE

Recently I happened upon some childhood snapshots that jostled loose memories and caused me to wonder, "How in the world did I get here?" *Here* started in rural, southeastern Pennsylvania. Centuries-old farms dotted a landscape filled with more horses than people. The population was such that eyebrows were raised when our post office's box numbers climbed into the triple digits.

It would be misleading of me, however, to portray my youth as that of a simple farm boy. My parents' trade — raising and racing thoroughbreds — was peopled with high rollers, cold betters, cool hustlers, hot walkers, and even the occasional honest horseman, all of them ladled from a cultural brew containing but one passion — fast horses. My father, lucky enough to own a few such horses, hauled me along to tracks up and down the East Coast. I remember breakfasts in Hialeah, Florida; furlong dogs for lunch at Delaware Park; and after-dinner ice-creams while the trotters pounded by under the lights at Saratoga, New York. Junkets away from the track included adventures in the Bahamas and Canada. By the age of eight I had eaten everything from French pâté to conch chowder, heard the loon's call and the fox huntsman's bugle, seen the Kentucky Derby, the turquoise waters of the Bahamas, and the cobalt blue skies of northern Canada.

While times spent on the road were full of adventure, time at home was a bit more sedate. Back in those days life was blissfully uncorrupted by today's modern media blitz, so for the most part entertainment was self-created, not presented to you. At an early age I discovered the countryside and it became my friend, mentor, and playground. A good day included exploring a rotten tree stump, peering into an abandoned nest, worrying some chattering gray squirrels, sampling wild berries, and inventorying the evening's batch of flickering lightning bugs. During those wanderings the whole world seemed wonderful.

Of course there were more conventional adventures. On Saturdays my dad and I headed out for the mail and Creamsicles, then other errands. We'd rattle over back roads in a rusted-out Willy's pickup fashioned with spasmodic, vacuum-driven windshield wipers and temperamental, thrill-inducing brakes. There was always time for chatter with neighbors or, in early July, for picking wine berries.

But, if truth be told, the local dump was for me the high point of those weekly excursions. There, free for the taking, was a treasure-trove of *National Geographic*, *Life*, and *Look* magazines, which I poured through the way other kids read comics books. To this day, John Dominis' startling and powerful images of East Africa's big cats, published in a series of late-Sixties *Life* issues, are etched in my memory. From the discarded journals sprouted a youthful dream to actually see all those places I could barely imagine.

So there you have it. Minds far wiser than mine could explain how the grown man I am today was fashioned from those youthful dreams and adventures, but it is safe to say that I was not destined for a desk job. From my current perspective I see how I was conditioned by my past to enjoy the solitude of the open road and to document the details of everyday life.

Let's pick up the story around my early thirties, when I was writing magazine articles for a living. After a while, to illustrate the articles, I taught myself photography. Wandering around outdoors with a camera turned out to be much more engaging than working indoors on a keyboard, so the tide began to turn.

The work of great photographers such as Paul Strand, Sam Abell, Bill Allard, Ernst Haas, and Elliot Porter have nurtured my photographic vision. Each is a master of the beautifully-crafted, enduring image that greets the eye, touches the soul, and expresses an intimate moment. Working on *Moments in Time* offered me an opportunity to present my style as it had evolved under the influences of these photographers.

Thinking of other influences, I must mention one more. Charles Kuralt, the acclaimed TV reporter and original host of "Sunday Morning," inspired me to pursue the oldest of art forms, storytelling. With his unique style and his insatiable curiosity, Kuralt convinced me that a good story, offered with passion and integrity, could entertain and teach in the most satisfying manner. And he taught me that there are good stories everywhere. If you sense a tinge of his soul in my work, well, good. Mr. Kuralt was my travel companion during the Utah adventure, encouraging me to look closer for those whispered nuances that define character. At times of uncertainly I heard his deep, rhythmic voice say to me, "You're doing just fine, Michael. Keep after this story, it's a good one. Just mosey along and look out the window. The pictures will find you."

Why Utah?

"Why Utah?" is a question I am often asked. I'd like to tell you a long and colorful story about how generations of Wickeses toiled away in Zion; about how it is my life's goal and destiny to tell this story. But only the destiny part would be true. Before starting *Moments In Time* I knew little about Utah.

This book was hatched out on a bus in New York City. My friend Bill Smith, a first-class New York photographer, was listening to me talk about my need to find a new project. I wanted a good story, rich in detail and character, that would give me lots of room to express some ideas and techniques I'd been developing. A book on Idaho, my home state, was considered but dismissed. "The less you know about a place," he said, "the more you're apt to sense the place's real character. Plus, you'll find stuff that the local photographers miss. How about a book on Utah?" It made sense at that moment on the bus, so I pointed my future toward The Beehive State.

By May 1st, my birthday, I was on the road, giddy with anticipation, driving highways, then smaller roads, and eventually nameless trails. In that way I was able to brush up close against the land, to meet the people, to find the rhythms. Helper, Moab, Bluff, Cedar Mesa — in short order I fell in love with the astounding beauty of Utah. And on I drove, and shot.

I discovered that Utah has a landscape unequaled in the West: stark salt flats, rugged red-rock country, graceful farmlands. And of course, mountains, sacred mountains — skied, climbed, hiked, explored — each teaming with enough wildlife to have forced Noah to order a second ark. I found that the cultural tapestry of Utah is quilted with Mormons, Gentiles, Native Americans, Hispanics, saints, sinners, and even a few scoundrels.

I met an agreeable mix of folks with names like Ada, Doke, Nino, Joe, Shirley, Darla, and White Crane. We shared Diet Cokes or iced-tea while we talked. "You betcha," was the usual answer to a request for assistance. These are the kind of folks you want around if your car dies. As they drive the back roads, one hand rests atop the steering wheel, always ready to wave.

AN INVITATION TO DANCE

It is May 1st, another birthday in Utah. Flaming Gorge hosts a sunrise challenge
match between a sullen storm and the rising sun. Stepping away from the view
camera, I sip hot chocolate gone cold and pat Calhoun, my old Gordon setter.
I know that this will be one of the last shots for the book.

Two days ago I was a guest at the ceremonial Noochew Bear Dance on
Nootuvweep — a Ute ceremony on Ute land, which is now the reservation. The
wife of the bear dance chief flicked her shawl at me, selecting me to dance.
Surprised, I mumbled something about not being Ute. She smiled and held out her
hand. "I have watched you move among our people," she said. "You belong here."

I'd like to think she was right, that I did belong there at the dance. And having
moved for a while among the people of Utah, I'd like to think that now
I belong here, too.

MICHAEL WICKES

D E S E R T

Among the Ancients

Rim rocks, near Delicate Arch

Previous spread: World of Speed, Bonneville Salt Flats

Plateau Lizard, Cedar Mesa

Eric Bjornstad, Moab

Previous spread: Spring Creek Canyon, near Cedar City

Zion National Park

Cedar Mesa, near Bluff

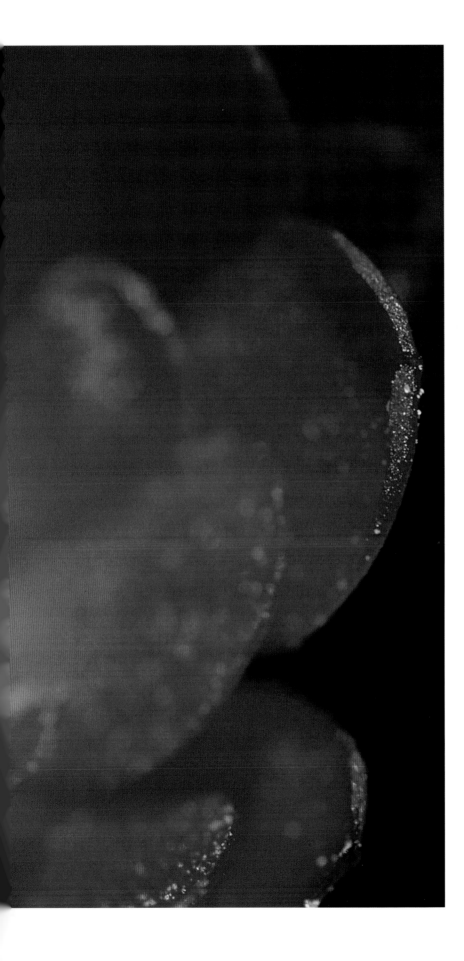

WILLIAM BLAKE

To see a World in a Grain of Sand

And Heaven in a Wild Flower,

Hold Infinity in the palm of your hand

And Eternity in an hour.

— Auguries of Innocence

Town hall, Virgin

Previous spread: Claret cup, Cedar Mesa

Southwestern Utah

Previous spread: Aspen leaf, Mill Canyon, near Moab

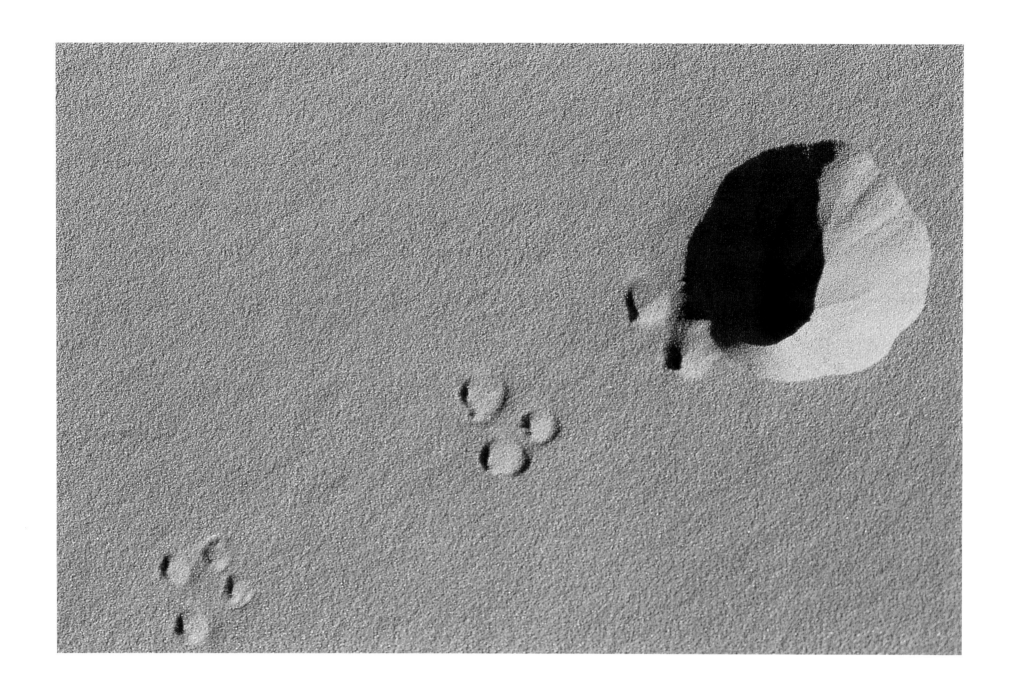

Coral Pink Sand Dunes, near Kanab

Wedge Overlook, near Castle Dale

Corey Perkins' stock, Cedar Mesa

EDWARD ABBEY

"Once upon a time, only a generation ago, they were horsemen,

nomads, keepers of flocks, painters in sand, weavers of wool,

artists in silver, dancers, singers of the Yei-bei-chei. . . . The

Navajo are people not personnel; nothing in their nature

or tradition has prepared them to adapt to the regimentation

of application forms and time clock."

North Window Arch, Arches National Park

Previous spread: Ada Benally (Dine, Navajo), Bluff

Red Canyon, near Bryce Canyon National Park

Anasazi ruin, Cedar Mesa

"Remember this moment always as a time that you saw the souls of those whose poetry and writing cover these walls. We have let you in. . . . Remember us."

— Grafton (ghost town in Utah), graffiti

Valley of the Gods, from Cedar Mesa

Previous spread: Anasazi rock art, Cedar Mesa

Mountain bikers, Moab

Next spread: Coral Pink Sand Dunes, near Kanab

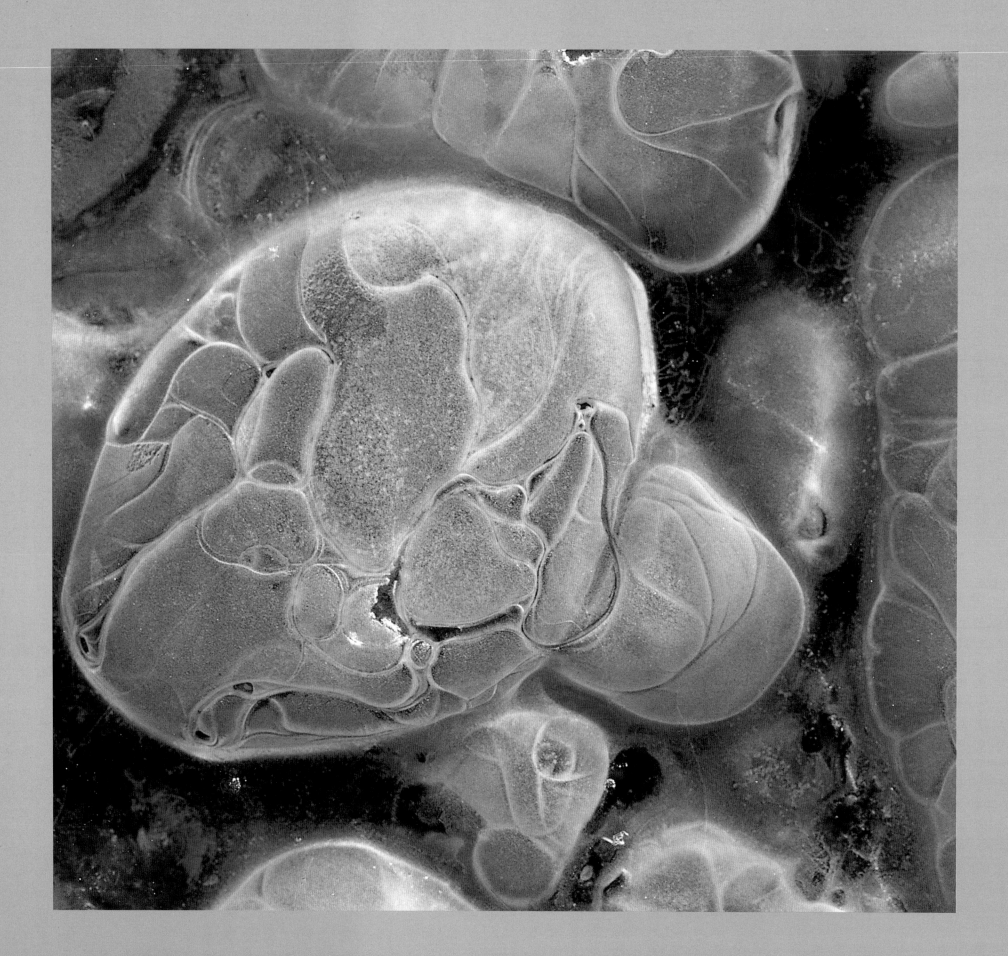

ALPINE

Into the Enchanted and Unknown

Beaver River

Previous spread: Tushar Mountains

Common merganser, Beaver River

Mountain goats, Tushar Mountains

Skiers at Park City

Previous spread: Snowboarder at Elk Meadows Ski Resort

Utah Olympic Park, Park City

Strawberry Reservoir, near Heber

EVERETT RUESS

"I have been one who loved the wilderness:

Swaggered and softly crept between the mountain peaks;

I listened long to the sea's brave music;

I sang my songs above the shriek of desert winds."

Flaming Gorge, from Canyon Rim

Previous spread: Yellow-headed blackbird, Ouray National Wildlife Refuge

Ruffed grouse, Mirror Lake Highway

Uinta Mountains, near Flaming Gorge

Drift boat, Flaming Gorge

Brown trout, Flaming Gorge

Kokanee salmon, near Strawberry Reservoir

Wasatch Range, near Sundance Resort

Sundance Farms, Heber

"A person's mind stretched by a new idea never goes back to

its original dimensions."

White Pine Lake, Logan Canyon

Previous spread: Mount Timpanogos, above Sundance Resort

Wasatch Range, above Altamont Campground

Hardware Ranch Wildlife Management Area

Elk, Hardware Ranch Wildlife Management Area

Next spread: White Pine Lake, Logan Canyon

F A R M

Where Once There Was Sage

Angus cattle, near Fillmore

Previous spread: Sorting sheep, Chew Ranch, near Vernal

Moving calves for branding, Chew Ranch, near Vernal

Flowell, near Fillmore

Sage grouse (male) on lek, near Minersville

Previous spread: Bailing hay, Flowell, near Fillmore

Near Eskdale

"I've learned that lying in the green grass of an empty field

makes you feel so good."

Burrowing Owl, Pine Valley, near Beryl

Previous spread: Water drop, Huntsville

Checkerspot butterfly, Pine Valley

Rancher, Chew Ranch, near Vernal

Sorting sheep, Chew Ranch, near Vernal

Car Hop Cafe, Fillmore

Franny's Barber Shop, Helper

Cove Fort

Dutch-oven cook-off, Virgin

Bear Dance, Ute Reservation

"Beauty is not discovered with the eye but with the soul."

Rodeo queens, Oakley Rodeo

Previous spread: July 4th parade, Oakley

Rodeo queen, Oakley Rodeo

Bull rider, Oakley Rodeo

Previous spread: Oakley Rodeo

Oakley

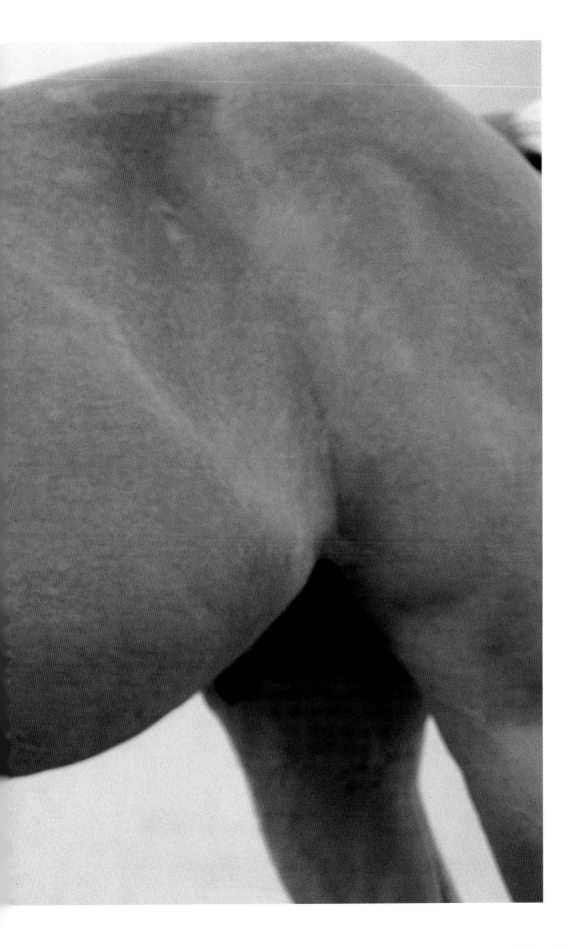

Oakley

Oakley

July 4th parade, Oakley

Oakley

July 4th parade, Oakley

Cheerleaders, Fillmore

Millard vs. Richfield varsity football, Fillmore

Next spread: J.V. football, Beaver

C I T Y

Taming the Wilderness

Ogden Raptors, minor league baseball, Ogden

Previous spread: July 4th fireworks at Ogden Raptors game, Ogden

July 4th fireworks, Ogden Raptors, minor league baseball, Ogden

LDS Temple, Salt Lake City

Lightning, near St. George

"In another moment, down went Alice after it [the Rabbit],

never once considering how in the world she was to get out again."

— Alice in Wonderland

Previous page and this spread: Center Stage Dance Studio, Orem

Page 136: Bridal store, Provo

Cedar waxwing, Heber

"Civilization is a limitless multiplication of unnecessary necessaries."

Alta Motel, Logan

Previous spread: Black Diamond, Salt Lake City

At the Lost Art Tattoo, Salt Lake City

Steiner Aquatic Center, Salt Lake City

Next spread: Great Salt Lake, near Saltair

Weber River, Ogden

Navajo Code Talker, West Valley

Previous spread: Avocet, Ogden Nature Center, Ogden

Pow-wow competition, Salt Lake City

Next spread: Dandelion, St. George.

The Photography

This assignment offered an exciting range of potential subjects, including wildlife, nature, people, and landscapes. Without a doubt, challenges arose from shifting between the different motifs, but any potential difficulties were offset by the stimulation and exhilaration that the variety afforded.

I traveled with an array of equipment. My core system is three Canon EOS bodies and lenses ranging in focal length from 20mm to 600mm. A Leica M6, a Nikonos, underwater housing, and a Toyo view camera were also stuffed into the Rover. To optimize the sharpness possible with modern optics, three different tripods and a monopod were used religiously. When necessary, I also used Metz, Leica, and Lumedyne strobes.

Most of these images were shot on either Fuji Sensia or Velvia. Low-light scenes were captured with Kodak E200 and Agfa RSX 200. Scala was selected for the black-and-whites.

What you see is what I shot. None of these images were manipulated by computer software except to insure an accurate transition from film to the printed paper. Each photograph is a truthful representation of reality.

Every image on these pages jostles loose a flood of memories for me. I hope these notes help you understand both the photography and the subjects.

MICHAEL WICKES

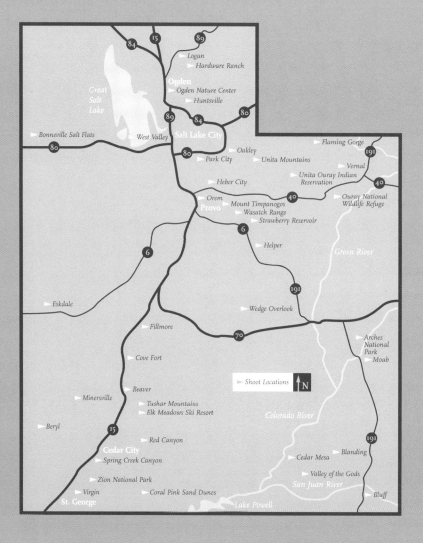

SHORT-HORNED GRASSHOPPER, ARCHES NATIONAL PARK
CANON EOS1N, 100MM, VELVIA

I can't look at this picture without thinking of Jiminy Cricket singing, "When you wish upon a star..." More than once, while I was a kid, these lyrics and Mr. Cricket's joyful spirit brightened an otherwise cloudy day.

WORLD OF SPEED, BONNEVILLE SALT FLATS
CANON EOS3, 20-35MM, FUJI 100

These races were staged about ten days after the 9/11 attack by terrorists. During a moment of silence observed for the victims, and then the singing of the national anthem, I was mesmerized by the powerfully expressive emotions etched on the faces of these motorheads, which dictated a respectful withdrawal of my cameras. There would be opportunities for pictures later in the day.

RIM ROCKS, NEAR DELICATE ARCH
LEICA M6, 35MM, FUJI 100

I picked a bad day to visit this beautiful arch. Not only was the scene disturbed by a mob of unruly high school students, but I learned that a well-known Utah photographer/instructor had lit a fire under the arch, burning the surrounding rock, in order to offer his pupils a unique lighting situation. This image brought me back to the simple beauty of the arch.

PLATEAU LIZARD, CEDAR MESA
CANON EOS3, 100MM, FUJI 100

It's hard to imagine southern Utah 150 million years ago, in the Jurassic period, when the climate was mild and moist. Here traipsed huge dinosaurs such as camarasaurus and stegosaurus, probably distant relatives to this little plateau lizard.

SPRING CREEK CANYON, NEAR CEDAR CITY
LEICA M6, 90MM, FUJI 100

This shot reminds me of Elliot Porter's photographs of the now-submerged Glen Canyon. His exquisite images are a valuable reminder of the consequences of the human footprint on southern Utah.

ERIC BJORNSTAD, MOAB
CANON EOS3, 100MM, FUJI 100

As dusk softened the jagged edges of Canyonlands, Eric and I watched two climbers descend Moses, a spire in the Park. I had noticed earlier that one of Eric's renowned guidebooks lay open on the seat of the climbers' battered car. After talking a while we agreed on three things. One, find a passion; two, follow it; and three, we needed some beer.

ZION NATIONAL PARK
TOYO 4X5, 65MM, VELVIA

I enjoy shooting winter landscapes. It's a time when the bone structure of the land is exposed, and there is always the possibility that the weather will be dramatic. This is one of the first landscapes that I have shot with a majority of the scene in the shade.

21

CEDAR MESA, NEAR BLUFF
CANON EOS3, 24MM TILT/SHIFT, VELVIA

This is the scene noted in the book's introduction. Edward Abbey was known to have camped on Cedar Mesa. It's said that a German launched himself in his car off the edge in a successful suicide attempt. Anasazi must have walked right through my camp site on their way to the mesa from the San Juan River below. This is where I met Utah.

22-23

CLARET CUP, CEDAR MESA
CANON EOS1N, 100MM, VELVIA

Art is often an exercise in subtraction. For this shot I wanted only tiny points of the flower in focus, so I let the rest fall soft and muted into the background.

24-25

TOWN HALL, VIRGIN
CANON EOS3, 500MM, FUJI 100

Perhaps only in Utah, and maybe the deep South, could a town pass an ordinance that requires a gun in every household, or one that bans employees of the United Nations. Those laws are on the books in Virgin and Laverkin, respectively. Democracy at its best and worst.

26-27

ASPEN LEAF, MILL CANYON, NEAR MOAB
CANON EOS1N, 100MM, VELVIA

Much of Utah's deserts are covered with cryptobiotic soil, a mix of bacteria, algae, lichens, fungi, and mosses. Although not always visually obvious, this fragile crust is an important desert component, creating a nest for seeds and capturing soil, water, and nutrients. It is important that we walk with care and stay on existing trails.

28-29

SOUTHWESTERN UTAH
LEICA M6, 35MM, FUJI 100

Initially, I decided not to cover controversial issues. However, when I saw the distinctive hairstyle and garb of this segment of the cultural landscape, I chose to include a tasteful portrait.

30-31

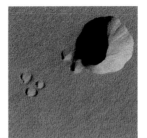

CORAL PINK SAND DUNES, NEAR KANAB
LEICA M6, 35MM, FUJI 100

In its larva stage the antlion digs a pit and calls it home. On the domestic agenda: wait for an insect to fall in, grab the doomed prey with pincer-like jaws, inject it with venom, and suck out the contents. The carcass is then flipped out of the pit. I'm not sure if these tracks are those of the eater or the eaten.

32

WEDGE OVERLOOK, NEAR CASTLE DALE
PENTAX 67, 45MM, FUJI 100

The vast expanses of sage steppe have been abused by various human disturbances, then invaded by introduced grasses from Europe and Asia that are ecologically inappropriate. Many land managers are concerned with the resulting degradation, but have found few realistic solutions. At least for now we still have the rich, aromatic scent of big sage to enjoy.

33

COREY PERKINS' STOCK, CEDAR MESA
CANON EOS3, 20-35MM, FUJI 100

Horses "say" a lot with the movement of their ears. Maybe humans need longer ones.

34-35

ADA BENALLY (DINE, NAVAJO), BLUFF
CANON EOS3, 100MM, FUJI 100

I wish there had been a way for the United States to become a nation without the hardships we heaped upon the Native Americans. It's difficult for me to read Western American history without feeling ashamed of our treatment of the environment and the indigenous people.

36-37

NORTH WINDOW ARCH, ARCHES NATIONAL PARK
LEICA M6, 35MM, FUJI 100

When I first started this book, I wanted to avoid photographing the already-cliched subjects of Utah, including smiley-faced powder skiers, and happy families cavorting in alpine meadows. This is my arch shot, and I like the way it portrays the wonder and magic of an arch without including one.

38

RED CANYON, NEAR BRYCE CANYON NATIONAL PARK
TOYO 4X5, 65MM, VELVIA

The well-known Bryce Canyon National Park is just up the road, but I found Red Canyon more interesting and certainly less documented. It's a shame that travelers often speed right by places like Red Canyon on the way to more popular destinations.

39

ANASAZI RUIN, CEDAR MESA

PENTAX 67, 45MM, FUJI 100

The Anasazi (Pueblo) carefully situated their dwellings so that the overhangs would keep the hot summer sun out, but allow the low-angle winter rays to warm the house all day long.

40-41

ANASAZI ROCK ART, CEDAR MESA

PENTAX 67, 45MM, FUJI 100

This is a duck-head petroglyph dating anywhere from 5000 BC to 500 AD. The early Basketmakers were no doubt intrigued by the duck's ability to swim above and below water, to fly and to migrate. The artist, probably Hopi or Zuni, was most likely a prehistoric ancestor of the Pueblo people of New Mexico and Arizona.

42-43

VALLEY OF THE GODS, FROM CEDAR MESA

CANON EOS3, 600MM, FUJI 100

Just after taking this image, I met two high school teachers from California. The conversation moved to public-lands grazing, a subject both teachers were opposed to. One said, "All ranchers who graze on public lands should be shot with an AK-47." I was appalled to hear this language from anyone, especially teachers.

44

MOUNTAIN BIKERS, MOAB

PENTAX 67, 45MM, FUJI 100

A proper campfire, and I don't mean a towering scorcher, welcomes both good conversation and thoughtful quiet.

45

CORAL PINK SAND DUNES, NEAR KANAB

TOYO 4X5, 65MM, VELVIA

Most of these graceful dunes are open to off-road vehicle use, so there's a good chance you'll be greeted by a screaming machine tearing over the sand. There is the occasional day when the off-roaders stay at home, leaving the delicate beauty to barefoot kids, poets, and photographers.

46-47

FROZEN ROCKS, ZION NATIONAL PARK

CANON EOS3, 100MM, FUJI 100

I am too much of a realist to think that my pictures will change the world. Still, I hope that this book will encourage a closer look at the details of everyday life.

48

TUSHAR MOUNTAINS

LEICA M6, 35MM, FUJI 100

I was having a bad day. The temperature lingered around zero, not counting the wind chill factor, and my head was pounding from the high altitude. The mountain goats I was looking for had moved away, probably south towards Mt. Holly. So I tried a few quick landscapes. Then, right after taking this shot, a screaming blast of wind knocked me to the ground. Just another day at the office.

50-51

BEAVER RIVER

PENTAX 67, 45MM, FUJI 100

I remember the absolute quiet of this scene. It was a windless morning and the cloudy sky, the fresh-fallen snow, and the murmur of trickling water all combined to create a surreal setting that was utterly peaceful.

52

COMMON MERGANSER, BEAVER RIVER

CANON EOS3, 500MM, FUJI 100

It is a wonderful experience to watch wildlife, and it's even better to watch up close and undetected. This merganser fished, preened, and puttered around for thirty minutes right in front of me.

53

MOUNTAIN GOATS, TUSHAR MOUNTAINS

CANON EOS3, 500MM, FUJI 100

These goats are an example of the many successful mountain goat introductions into areas where they were not originally indigenous. Unlike most feral (wild) horses, these mountain goats do not compete with native species, nor have they adversely impacted the rangeland.

54-55

SNOWBOARDER AT ELK MEADOWS SKI RESORT

CANON EOS3, 20-35MM, FUJI 100

Take almost a foot of new snow and add a handful of bored mountain employees with shovels and plywood. The result is a jump that launches them, flipping and twisting, into an April sky. The roars of laughter and applause subsided when a grumbly mountain manager arrived and shut down the fun.

56-57

SKIERS AT PARK CITY

CANON EOS3, 20-35MM, FUJI 100

Photographing kids and bright colors — it's almost cheating.

58

UTAH OLYMPIC PARK, PARK CITY

CANON EOS3, 500MM, FUJI 100

No image, still or moving, can do justice to the aerial display of these skiers. They launch as high as seventy feet, then fall earthward, all the time twisting and flipping with absolute precision. Then they land on their skis. Most of the time.

59

STRAWBERRY RESERVOIR, NEAR HEBER

LEICA M6, 35MM, FUJI 100

When I was young, local kids would meet at frozen ponds for informal hockey games and, later, a bonfire with hot dogs and hot chocolate. This girl shrieked with fear and joy as she inched her way out across the ice. She'd just discovered a trout swimming under the ice.

60-61

YELLOW-HEADED BLACKBIRD, OURAY NATIONAL WILDLIFE REFUGE

CANON EOS3, 600MM, FUJI 100

Who could complain about spending the night charmed by a chorus of coots, spring peepers, and yellow-headed blackbirds? Sound, more then imagery, reminds me of a time and place. I remember this night every time I hear any of these three species.

62-63

FLAMING GORGE, FROM CANYON RIM OVERLOOK

CANON EOS3, 300MM, VELVIA

This is one of the last pictures I shot for the book. That it is unclear whether this is a sunrise or sunset reflects my mood at the time.

64

RUFFED GROUSE, MIRROR LAKE HIGHWAY

CANON EOS3, 300MM, FUJI 100

At dusk and dawn in the spring, the male ruffed grouse will perch on a log or rock and beat the air with its wings, sounding like a very old piston-engine water pump. This action is called drumming and it is repeated about every ten minutes for an hour or so to attract a mate. A loose translation of the bird's Latin name is "wild bull with umbrella neck feathers."

65

UINTA MOUNTAINS, NEAR FLAMING GORGE

TOYO 4X5, 65MM, VELVIA

I just barely caught a glimpse of water through the trees and decided to pull over. It turned out to be an unremarkable pond. But the sun setting directly over the trees and the log in the foreground created a scene worth capturing.

66-67

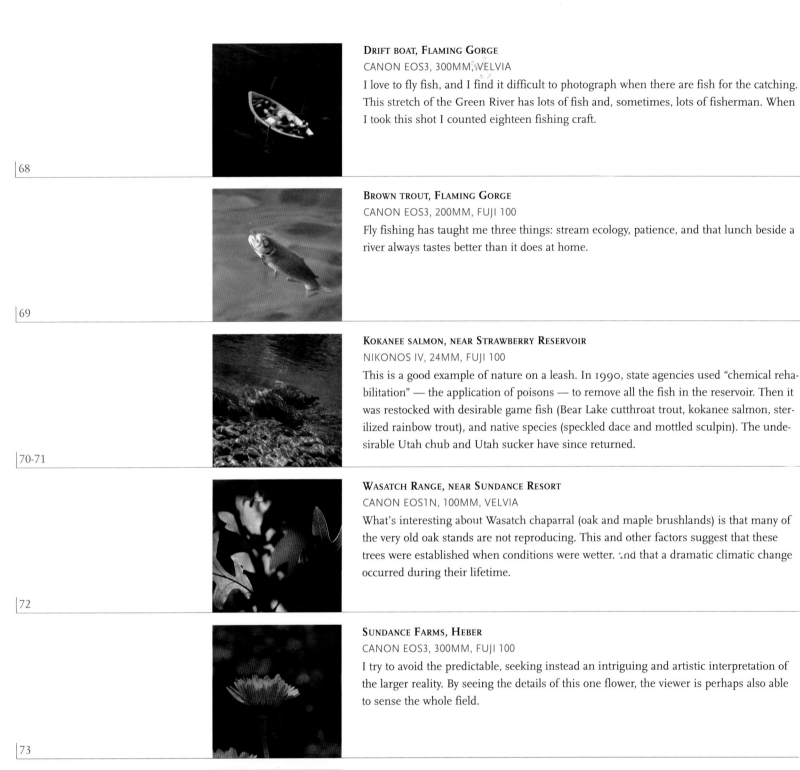

Drift boat, Flaming Gorge
CANON EOS3, 300MM, VELVIA

I love to fly fish, and I find it difficult to photograph when there are fish for the catching. This stretch of the Green River has lots of fish and, sometimes, lots of fisherman. When I took this shot I counted eighteen fishing craft.

68

Brown trout, Flaming Gorge
CANON EOS3, 200MM, FUJI 100

Fly fishing has taught me three things: stream ecology, patience, and that lunch beside a river always tastes better than it does at home.

69

Kokanee salmon, near Strawberry Reservoir
NIKONOS IV, 24MM, FUJI 100

This is a good example of nature on a leash. In 1990, state agencies used "chemical rehabilitation" — the application of poisons — to remove all the fish in the reservoir. Then it was restocked with desirable game fish (Bear Lake cutthroat trout, kokanee salmon, sterilized rainbow trout), and native species (speckled dace and mottled sculpin). The undesirable Utah chub and Utah sucker have since returned.

70-71

Wasatch Range, near Sundance Resort
CANON EOS1N, 100MM, VELVIA

What's interesting about Wasatch chaparral (oak and maple brushlands) is that many of the very old oak stands are not reproducing. This and other factors suggest that these trees were established when conditions were wetter, and that a dramatic climatic change occurred during their lifetime.

72

Sundance Farms, Heber
CANON EOS3, 300MM, FUJI 100

I try to avoid the predictable, seeking instead an intriguing and artistic interpretation of the larger reality. By seeing the details of this one flower, the viewer is perhaps also able to sense the whole field.

73

Mount Timpanogos, above Sundance Resort
CANON EOS3, 300MM, VELVIA

When I first arrived here the sky was blue and the scene was picture-postcard perfect, which did not interest me. Luckily some clouds drifted in, adding more drama.

74-75

WHITE PINE LAKE, LOGAN CANYON
CANON EOS3, 24MM TILT/SHIFT, VELVIA
As soon as I saw this scene, I thought of the work of Sam Abell, one of my favorite photographers. I tried a shot with the log running vertically through the middle of the frame — very Abell. It didn't quite work, so I tried other framings, this being the most interesting.

76

WASATCH RANGE, ABOVE ALTAMONT CAMPGROUND
CANON EOS3, 200MM, FUJI 100
I laughed with this guy about the fact that a multi-thousand-dollar mountain bike does not endow the rider with either strength or skill. He clearly had both.

77

HARDWARE RANCH WILDLIFE MANAGEMENT AREA
CANON EOS1N, 100MM, VELVIA
Ultimately, I have to make pictures for myself. If I consider the opinions of others, doubt and uncertainty might replace instinct and creativity.

78

ELK, HARDWARE RANCH WILDLIFE MANAGEMENT AREA
CANON EOS3, 500MM, FUJI 100
Before us white folk got started in America, there were ten million elk scattered through all but four of the current states. Folklore incorrectly says that elk were driven up into the mountains; the truth is that it was elk in remote locations, and those protected in Yellowstone National Park, that escaped the guns of man. The rest lost their lives and habitat.

79

WHITE PINE LAKE, LOGAN CANYON
CANON EOS1N, 100MM, VELVIA
Whenever I get stuck trying to find a picture, I rely on my old standby, a 100mm close-up lens, and I focus on the details: hands, eyes, leaves, bugs, etc. I find the world fascinating at this scale.

80-81

CORRAL, NEAR BLANDING
CANON EOS3, 100MM, FUJI 100
Sometimes I talk out loud when I'm working. One time near Pierre, South Dakota, I was lying in the grass photographing a rattlesnake. Unbeknownst to me, a couple walked up behind me and overheard me discussing an "attitude problem" with the snake. I sat up just as they spun around and hurriedly left without saying a word.

82

SORTING SHEEP, CHEW RANCH, NEAR VERNAL

LEICA M6, 35MM, FUJI 100

For this shot I exposed many frames with the hope that just one might work. It is the sheep's sharp face and the boy's dark sweatshirt that anchor this blurred image.

84-85

ANGUS CATTLE, NEAR FILLMORE

CANON EOS3, 200MM, FUJI 100

Many of the New Westerners would be content to see the Old Western lifestyle fade away. Certainly it is debatable whether replacing an alfalfa field with a subdivision, or a herd of sheep with a herd of mountain bikers or ATV's, is really an improvement. Still, both camps need to get together and agree on a plan to lessen our impact on the land. Wishful thinking, but I have hope.

86

MOVING CALVES FOR BRANDING, CHEW RANCH, NEAR VERNAL

LEICA M6, 35MM, FUJI 100

Doke Chew is as thin and wiry as a throttle cable, and just about as talkative. One thing he did talk about was how his granddad Doug bought the Chew Ranch on the day Pearl Harbor was bombed. In this day of parents too busy to be parents, it's great to see three generations of Chews working and eating together.

87

FLOWELL, NEAR FILLMORE

LEICA M6, 90MM, FUJI 100

Originally, I didn't like this shot because none of the subjects were looking at the camera or doing anything interesting. With time it grew on me. Maybe that's because, as a viewer, I'm curious about what these three are thinking and seeing.

88-89

BAILING HAY, FLOWELL, NEAR FILLMORE

CANON EOS3, 600MM, FUJI 100

Farming is solitary work, often lonely and boring. The farmer in this picture, Neil Ashton, told me this. He was thankful that his retired dad was around to offer help, companionship, and a little fatherly advice.

90-91

SAGE GROUSE (MALE) ON LEK, NEAR MINERSVILLE

CANON EOS3, 600MM, FUJI 100

The sage grouse could become the next "spotted owl" for western public lands. A variety of human factors have caused a continuous decline in the bird's numbers, which in turn has triggered a call for dramatic changes in habitat management. This might force some people to say bye bye to moo moo and bleat bleat.

92

NEAR ESKDALE
LEICA M6, 35MM, SCALA

Badlands, Empty Quarter, Starvation Canyon — these are geographical nicknames that could be aptly applied to much of rugged and desolate western Utah. It is amazing that so many have tried to live on this land, generation after generation, and that many still keep on trying.

93

WATER DROP, HUNTSVILLE
CANON EOS1N, 100MM, VELVIA

This dewy field at dawn seemed to offer a bonanza of easy dew-drop shots. However, it soon proved difficult to find droplets that were big enough to photograph. Then, whenever I got close, they would fall to the ground. This one image was obtained after two soggy hours of cautiously stalking the dangerous and elusive dew drop.

94-95

BURROWING OWL, PINE VALLEY, NEAR BERYL
CANON EOS3, 600MM, FUJI 100

After this wonderful little owl took off, I found some feathers from another one that had been shot or eaten. I gathered (illegally) a few of them, thinking they'd make a good gift. A Cree/Cherokee friend warned me that for many Native Americans owls are harbingers of evil, and suggested I learn more about a tribe's beliefs before visiting them.

96

CHECKERSPOT BUTTERFLY, PINE VALLEY
CANON EOS3, 100MM, FUJI 100

As a kid I spent lots of time wandering around the woods, fields, and streams on my parents' farm in Pennsylvania, puttering. It was not a land of grand vistas, like those you see in the West, so I grew to appreciate the short views and the small details. I am still quite content to just putter around any old wild someplace.

97

RANCHER, CHEW RANCH, NEAR VERNAL
LEICA M6, 35MM, FUJI 100

When I first met Dean he was alone working cattle in the rain, beautifully lit with a soft, dusk light. But I got so busy chatting with him that I completely forgot to pull out my cameras. Luckily, I was able to spend the next two days with him and his family, and I remembered to stop talking and start taking pictures.

98-99

SORTING SHEEP, CHEW RANCH, NEAR VERNAL
LEICA M6, 35MM, FUJI 100

A day or two with a ranch family like the Chews would dispel anyone's illusions about the romance of cowboy'n. They work from dawn to past dusk, often performing difficult, dangerous, and dirty tasks over and over again. Many folks would rather look like a cowboy than be one.

100-101

CAR HOP CAFE, FILLMORE
CANON EOS3, 20-35MM, FUJI 100

While waiting for her husband, Jennifer told me a little about her life in Fillmore. Married right out of high school, she never went to college and has waitressed at the Car Hop ever since she was fifteen. Her mom pressured her to have kids and at nineteen she's expecting her first child. On the way out she waved goodbye and said, "See ya, hun."

102

FRANNY'S BARBER SHOP, HELPER
CANON EOS3, 20-35MM, FUJI 100

If you want to get the pulse of a small town, hang out in the barber shop. Everybody talks to everybody and the gossip is hot. Politics, sports, romance, crime — all topics are covered with enthusiasm and embellishment. The haircut is seven bucks, the news is free.

103

COVE FORT
LEICA M6, 90MM, FUJI 100

I was drawn to the way this old glass interpreted the light inside the room, and I liked what it did to the scene outside. Someday, I will do a photographic study using this glass.

104-105

DUTCH-OVEN COOK-OFF, VIRGIN
LEICA M6, 35MM, FUJI 100

Dutch-oven cook-offs conjure up a vision of blackened pots filled with chiles and heavy stews. On the contrary, the gourmets at this competition prepared wondrous dishes including breads, desserts, and mouth-watering main courses. After the judging was over, for five bucks spectators could sample the entries. Yum!

106

BEAR DANCE, UTE RESERVATION
LEICA M6, 35MM, FUJI 100

The Bear Dance, one of the oldest Ute ceremonies, honors the arrival of spring. Traditionally these events were (and still are) organized so that the scattered families and bands could socialize, trade goods, meet potential mates, make hunting plans, and have fun.

107

JULY 4TH PARADE, OAKLEY
CANON EOS3, 20-35MM, FUJI 100

As a rule, I try not to surprise people when taking their picture. In this case, I liked the middle queen's expression, and the guy in the background near the pickup.

108-109

171

RODEO QUEENS, OAKLEY RODEO
CANON EOS3, 100MM, FUJI 100
Queening is a recognized pursuit throughout the West. Cowboy hats, fast horses, lots of lipstick, shiny sequins, big hair, and that special, flat-handed rotating-wrist wave — all of which make for great photo subjects.

110

RODEO QUEEN, OAKLEY RODEO
CANON EOS3, 100MM, FUJI 100
A horse would have added another interesting dimension to the portrait, but I was too dazzled by this queen's golden locks to think of it. That's the big difference between photography and writing. Words can be edited, but there's no fixing a picture.

111

OAKLEY RODEO
LEICA M6, 35MM, AGFA RSX200
Over the hill from quiet little Oakley lies the upscale, gentrified resort of Park City. Inevitably, that lifestyle will creep toward Oakley, push up taxes and land values, and eventually drive out the ranchers and other long-time locals.

112-113

BULL RIDER, OAKLEY RODEO
LEICA M6, 35MM, FUJI 100
At a rodeo, the atmosphere behind the chutes is intense. This is no place for a yahoo with a camera. Fortunately, these bull and bronc riders welcomed me into their camp. My secret: do not look and act like a geek, no flashes, nod when making eye contact. And chew.

114

OAKLEY
CANON EOS3, 20-35MM, FUJI 100
I think it was this gal who later in the day got dumped hard off her horse. When she picked herself up she had tears in her eyes and a mouthful of dirt, but her fluttering grin signaled that she was ok.

115

OAKLEY
CANON EOS3, 100MM, FUJI 100
I remember this young lady as very serious and dedicated. Her younger sister was a bit more light-hearted. Sometimes I wish I could look a decade into the future to see the adult version of these kids.

116-117

OAKLEY

CANON EOS3, 200MM, FUJI 100

An ancient scribe named Jean de la Bruyere said, "Children enjoy the present because they have neither a past, nor a future."

118

JULY 4TH PARADE, OAKLEY

CANON EOS3, 20-35MM, FUJI 100

This type of layered composition has taken me a long time to "see," much less execute. I look for a dominant foreground object (i.e. the two girls) and layers of supporting information (the other two people, the pickup), in order to create a multifaceted scene through which the eye and mind can wander.

119

OAKLEY

CANON EOS3, 200MM, FUJI 100

Many portraits are creative but lack character, presenting details but no passion. While it's easy to offer this critique, it's difficult to overcome it. My solution: try to create a rapport with the subject, and shoot lots of film.

120

JULY 4TH PARADE, OAKLEY

CANON EOS3, 20-35MM, FUJI 100

I have neither the talent nor interest to pose, outfit, or apply make-up to a person. I figure that with patience and a little luck I can make good pictures, occasionally a very good one.

121

CHEERLEADERS, FILLMORE

CANON EOS3, 20-35MM, FLASH, KODAK E200

High school sports, like church, are one of the vital threads in the weave of small town life, offering students important skills and giving families an opportunity to socialize and eat a good hot dog. Faltering hometown economies force many of these kids to leave for college or work in cities. Few return; some wish they had never left.

122

MILLARD VS. RICHFIELD VARSITY FOOTBALL, FILLMORE

CANON EOS3, 200MM, FLASH, KODAK E200

I have a theory about why Utah has produced so many great football players. The city streets are usually a whopping 132 feet across, wide enough to turn around an oxen train. Crossing this expanse requires superior footwork, unflinching nerves, and a sprinter's speed. By the way, Fillmore's season record was 13-0, and they won the state championship!

123

J.V. FOOTBALL, BEAVER
LEICA M6, 35MM, FUJI 100
Right after I took this shot, a rather large cop hauled me into his squad car, called in backup, and accused me of using an "X-ray camera to photograph little boys." An X-ray camera the size of a point-&-shoot (it was a Leica M6) — did he think I was Superman? Anyway, after showing him my credentials he sulked away. Oh, the perils of the road.

124-125

AT THE LOST ART TATTOO, SALT LAKE CITY
CANON EOS3, 100MM, FUJI 100
This is my favorite portrait from the book. I take no credit for any technical or creative mastery here. It's just that Roger is so cool, and he very naturally posed himself.

126 AND 147

JULY 4TH FIREWORKS AT OGDEN RAPTORS GAME, OGDEN
LEICA M6, 35MM, FUJI 100
A prominent spectator with a private, fieldside box bellowed advice to everyone on the ballfield. When he directed his counsel towards me ("Hey fella, get a picture of . . ."), it was time to relocate.

128-129

OGDEN RAPTORS, MINOR LEAGUE BASEBALL, OGDEN
LEICA M6, 35MM, FUJI 100
Minor league baseball offers kids like Kyle Rhode a great opportunity to watch and even meet professional ballplayers. Ogden, Salt Lake City, and Provo all have teams. Ticket prices for games run from free to $10.00, so an outing to the yard is good fun and a great deal.

130-131

JULY 4TH FIREWORKS, OGDEN RAPTORS, MINOR LEAGUE BASEBALL, OGDEN
LEICA M-6, 35MM, FUJI 100
July 4th is a wonderful holiday: barbeque, fireworks, parades, rodeos, fairs. Who could ask for more fun and better photographic subjects?

132

LDS TEMPLE, SALT LAKE CITY
CANON EOS3, 200MM, FUJI 100
The temple is imposing and impressive, but more importantly the throng of pilgrims, locals, and staff is warm and welcoming.

133

LIGHTNING, NEAR ST. GEORGE

CANON EOS3, 300MM, FUJI 100

Where I grew up in Pennsylvania, lightning was a wonderful and dangerous occurrence. Living in the West, I miss it. I honestly don't remember much about taking this shot. I was sleeping in the back of my car somewhere north of St. George when the storm woke me up. I tumbled out into the night, shot three frames, and then jumped back in my car when the lightning closed in like artillery fire.

134-135

BRIDAL STORE, PROVO

LEICA M6, 35MM, FUJI 100

Underneath the excitement and anticipation, this young woman seemed sobered by her time in front of the mirror. Maybe she had caught a glimpse of her mother as a younger woman, or maybe she'd been able to see her life as a Mormon wife unfold before her.

136-137

CENTER STAGE DANCE STUDIO, OREM

LEICA M6, 35MM, FUJI 100

Classes at this studio ranged from classic ballet (. . .and one and two and. . .) to break dancing. The students ranged from gangly beginners to gifted athletes. Requesting anonymity, one teenage boy admitted that he was mainly interested in the girls in his class.

138-139

CENTER STAGE DANCE STUDIO, OREM

LEICA M6, 35MM, FUJI 100

I am aware of two "edges" in a photographic scene. First there are the elements around the edges, or borders, of the viewfinder, which may be important to the story. The second is that edge of time that exists between peak activities. Here is an introspective moment, an edge, between rehearsals.

140-141

CEDAR WAXWING, HEBER

CANON EOS3, 500MM, FUJI 100

Here is another wildlife shot made in the midst of humanity. A group of chattering waxwings were gobbling up juniper berries outside my motel room one morning. In spite of the background clamor of rush hour traffic, I was able to enjoy these beautiful little birds.

142

BLACK DIAMOND, SALT LAKE CITY

CANON EOS3, 20-35MM, FLASH, KODAK E200

Dennis is a serious guy and rightfully so. He works on quality control for Black Diamond, a climbing equipment manufacturer. After a while in the shop I was able to coax a smile out of him by referring to him as a "cam stud."

143-144

ALTA MOTEL, LOGAN
CANON EOS3, 100MM, FUJI 100

I always try to find an older, non-chain motel when I'm on the road. You know, the ones offering erratic heaters, fans instead of air-conditioners, TVs with maybe two channels, and real cotton sheets. Alta, shown in this picture, owns one such little motel. I like pictures that simultaneously portray a mixture of emotions, especially happiness and sadness, and I see this in Alta's cheerful but lonely face. I know that Alta misses her deceased husband.

146

STEINER AQUATIC CENTER, SALT LAKE CITY
CANON A2, UNDERWATER HOUSING, 20-35MM, FUJI 100

This woman left her indoor aerobics class and braved the teeth-chattering cold water of the outdoor pool in order to help me make this image. I think the ripples on the water were created by our shivering.

148-149

GREAT SALT LAKE, NEAR SALTAIR
CANON EOS3, 20-35MM, FUJI 100

At the Great Salt Lake I had hoped to make an image of some kids floating in the buoyant water. Unfortunately, hardly anyone swims in the lake anymore. Just to the left of the scene a female spoonbill duck lay dying in the rocks. I considered both photographing and euthanizing her, but opted to let nature takes its course.

150-151

WEBER RIVER, OGDEN
CANON EOS3, 300MM, FLASH, FUJI 100

Marc Munson, a dairyman near Duchesne, told me, "Where the water flows, so goes the history of Utah. What the pioneers really learned how to do was to move water a long ways." To this day, one can find throughout Utah remnants of ditches, canals, and aqueducts laboriously built to achieve this goal.

152-153

AVOCET, OGDEN NATURE CENTER, OGDEN
CANON EOS3, 600MM, FUJI 100

It was my intention to make most of the nature and wildlife images for this book in locations that were easily accessible to lots of people. This little pond at the Nature Center was busy with avocets, stilts, and other waterfowl. Looking to my right I could see a herd of mule deer and, farther on, a juvenile detention center.

154-155

NAVAJO CODE TALKER, WEST VALLEY
CANON EOS3, 100MM, FUJI 100

Allan June is one of the original twenty-nine Navajo Code Talkers, and the only one to have left the military service ranked as a sergeant. About going to Hollywood to view the opening of "Wind Talker" with the film's star, Nicholas Cage, he said that although it was entertaining, the movie was an inaccurate representation of the real events.

156

Pow-wow competition, Salt Lake City

CANON EOS3, 200MM, FLASH, KODAK E200

Pow-wows are intertribal gatherings, part competition, part social time. The singers play a huge, shared drum and sing traditional songs. Dancers are divided by age, region of tribe, and outfit style. Remember to always walk around the perimeter of the sacred circle, never across it.

157

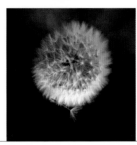

Dandelion, St. George

CANON EOS1N, 100MM, VELVIA

Someone once said that the only difference between a weed and a flower is judgment. Even the lowly dandelion deserves a closer look.

158-159

Photo by Michelle Daubert

W I C K E S

M I C H A E L

Michael Wickes, a native of southeastern Pennsylvania, lives in Hailey, Idaho. A self-taught photographer, he developed his photographic skills documenting horses and the horse-racing culture. From there his interests broadened to include wildlife, lifestyle, landscape, travel, and adventure. His work has carried him through many regions of the United States as well as Mexico, The Bahamas, Bolivia, France, England, Kenya, and India. Michael has published his images and writing in numerous magazines and books as well as corporate publications. His stock imagery is presented through The Image Works and Bruce Coleman. He has shared his skills and passion for photography through teaching and assistance to various non-profit organizations.